The Two Tasks

A BGC Monograph

the Two Wo Tasks

Charles Malik

Cornerstone Books
Westchester, Illinois

*This address was delivered during dedication
ceremonies for the Billy Graham Center at
Wheaton College in September 1980.
Opinions expressed are those of the author
and do not necessarily reflect the position
of the Center or the College.*

A BGC Monograph

*First printing, 1980.
Printed in the United States of America.*

ISBN 89107-212-8

Contents

Preface

AMERICAN HIGHER EDUCATION began with reverence for the Bible as the very Word of God, and with a concern for lost souls. The first advanced educational institution in the Colonies, Harvard College, was founded in 1646 with this chartered purpose: "Every one shall consider the main end of his life and studies to know God and Jesus Christ which is eternal life."

Even as late as 1890, one of the leaders in establishing the University of Chicago described his aspirations for that school: "An institution . . . loyal to Christ and his Church, employing none but Christians in any department of instruction; a school not only evangelical but evangelistic, seeking to bring every student to Jesus Christ as Lord."

Today, however, secularized and agnostic perspec-

7

tives seem to dominate many academic communities. Young people are graduated from otherwise excellent programs in the liberal arts and sciences that provide them with no sense of direction for their lives. They lack a values-based world view that gives meaning to being human, and that can motivate and guide them in service to God and humanity.

However, education can be truly ''higher'' only if it persistently explores the supernatural dimension. In the providence of God, certain schools have been raised up in the last century or more to preserve American education's founding tradition of combining faith with learning. Most of these schools, such as Wheaton College, meet all the rigorous academic standards that entitle them to full accreditation by the professional agencies. Their faculty members hold advanced degrees from major graduate institutions. Their students generally stand high in honors lists, and go out to assume effective leadership roles in society. Christian higher education, consequently, keeps reminding other colleges and universities that learning that addresses the ''whole'' person and specifically includes spiritual concerns best prepares students to meet the demands of contemporary life.

At the same time that Christian schools maintain intellectual respectability, therefore, they forthrightly emphasize spiritual accountability. Far from being incongruous, it makes eminently good sense to establish a research center for world evangelization within the structure of a Christian liberal arts college. No matter what a student's major field of study may be, it is constantly emphasized that Christ's command to make disciples of all nations gives motive power to life's vocations.

While that principle is clear, its outworking is not simple. The Billy Graham Center at Wheaton College is both dedicated to the principle and committed to working it out. The dedicatory address by Charles Habib Malik, reproduced in the following pages, stirred us as we listened to its forceful delivery on September 13, 1980. The destiny of this school, clearly envisioned in its founding in 1860, is soundly reaffirmed in Dr. Malik's challenge. We do face a double task. Together with all believers in Christ, we serve under a mandate to preach the Gospel to every creature, to evangelize the world. Beyond that, as our special calling by the Lord, we instruct and discipline young Christian minds to interpret and apply God's Word of truth to every aspect of life, personal and social.

The two tasks of which Dr. Malik speaks, however, are not separate and simply parallel. Rather, they comprise a unity whose inseparably intertwined elements transmit the saving power of God in the energy of the Holy Spirit to the heart of humanity. The task of evangelism contributes an eternal significance to the task of education. The task of education gives immediate significance to the task of evangelism.

In working out our understanding of Wheaton's heightened responsibilities, we purpose to seek instruction as well as to give it. We want to listen to fellow

Christians who can speak to us out of their own cherished traditions and from their own substantial convictions. Even as we firmly adhere to the beliefs and practices that have brought God's blessing to Wheaton for 120 years, we acknowledge the diversity of His dealings with His children, and we long to contribute our share to the unity of believers for which Jesus prayed.

In a spirit of learning and serving side by side, then, we commend this eloquent statement by Dr. Malik to our brothers and sisters in Christ.

Hudson T. Armerding
President,
Wheaton College

Foreword

THERE HAVE BEEN TIMES in my ministry when I felt that university campuses might well be among the most fruitful fields for evangelism. In visits to some fifty nations, I have found students to be attentive, and usually respectful, listeners to Gospel preaching. In spite of some superficial collegiate fads, they are basically involved in the search for self-understanding, for a view of life that makes sense, and for a useful role in society. Without knowing it, in many cases, they long for a personal fulfillment that can be found in Christ as nowhere else.

What is true of students is true of professors as well. However, like Nicodemus, many of them are not open about their quest. Encumbered in some ways by their academic degrees and scholarly activities, and by

11

the professional reputations to be maintained, they seem embarrassed to admit that spectres of ignorance, anxiety, and despair often invade their wakeful nights. The perpetual need to appear knowledgeable and self-assured before their students wears them thin.

When I ponder what such students and teachers say to me, I can see three main explanations for their "rejecting Christianity," as we put it.

First, many are reacting against an unsatisfying encounter with something that passes for Christianity in their thinking. Some man-made caricature has obscured Christ for them. Some grotesque methodology or heretical doctrine confuses them regarding an authentic biblical faith. If they have heard about forgiveness and peace and joy to be discovered in knowing Jesus, they discount its credibility because some "Christians" of their acquaintance apparently don't have it.

Second, many self-styled intellectuals are agnostic when it comes to religion, even though they may be very trusting in other areas of knowledge. In a self-contradictory way, they pursue selected kinds of knowledge, but close their minds against other kinds, including the spiritual. Not only do they not "make room for mystery," as Dr. A. W. Tozer phrased it, but also they reject actual evidence when it does not conform to their preconceived definitions.

Third, far too many of our brightest young men and women today have lost hope. Worsening global conditions threaten their future realization of present dreams. What is the use of all their efforts, they wonder, if a

12

madman might press a button that would atomize the human race. Or, what will their hard-earned Ph.D. degrees matter if the fabric of society is in shreds? Against all that gloom, Christianity's promise of a heaven hereafter strikes many intellectuals as beside the point.

Because these and other issues create a particular challenge in bringing the Gospel to bear on the seekers for truth in our schools, I believe that Christian intellectuals face a special evangelistic mandate. As Dr. Malik so forcefully argues in these pages, in our zeal to "save souls," we must not default in the battle for people's minds. We must proclaim a Gospel for the *whole* person. We must take seriously the biblical injunction to bring every *thought* into captivity to Christ.

In our Christian colleges and universities today is the vanguard of leadership—teachers and students—who must advance Christ's claim on the mind. Let there be no mistake about the job to be done. The summons is not to make biblical Christianity intellectually respectable; great thinkers of the ages in all fields already testify overwhelmingly that it is. The call, rather, is to confront this generation's scholars with the staggering Christian claim: in Christ Jesus the Lord, Son of God and Savior of men, is the Truth they all are seeking. The Christian faith is a norm for all disciplines, a light on the unknown as well as the known, and the ultimate key to human existence and experience.

True intellectuals are humble people because they know how hard it is to learn. They will not be impatient or overbearing toward others. As Christian scholars minister to their associates in secular settings, therefore, they bring not only the knowledge of Christ, but His Spirit as well. The universities then will become evangelized in the best sense: not by intellectual arguments alone, convincing as they might be; not by sermons on God's redeeming grace alone, imperative as they are. Instead, the task will be accomplished by the Truth of Christ spoken in the Love of Christ, by humble learners whose Master is Lord of all.

Billy Graham

The Two Tasks

Introduction

I SPEAK TO YOU as a Christian. Jesus Christ is my Lord and God and Savior and Song day and night. I can live without food, without drink, without sleep, without air, but I cannot live without Jesus. Without Him I would have perished long ago. Without Him and His church reconciling man to God the world would have perished long ago. I live in and on the Bible for long hours every day. The Bible is the source of every good thought and impulse I have. In the Bible God Himself, the Creator of everything from nothing, speaks to me and to the world directly, about Himself, about ourselves, and about His will for the course of events and for the consummation of history. And believe me, not a day passes without my crying from the bottom of my heart, "Come, Lord Jesus!" I know He is coming with

Glory to judge the living and the dead, but in my impatience I sometimes cannot wait, and I find myself in my infirmity crying with David, "How long, Lord?" And I know His Kingdom shall have no end.

I apologize for this personal witness and I know you will take it with a charitable heart.

1

NOTHING IS AS IMPORTANT in the world today as for the Christians of America to grasp their historic opportunities and prove themselves equal to them.

I say "the Christians," but I must add also "the Jews," because what is fatefully at stake today is the highest spiritual values of the Judaeo-Christian tradition. If the highest Christian values are overturned, so will the highest Jewish values.

Perhaps never since the Twelve Disciples and Saint Paul has any group of Christians been burdened by Providence itself with the responsibilities now devolving upon the Christians of America.

By "Christians" I mean at once the Protestants, the Catholics, and the Orthodox. The intensity of conviction, suffering, and witness being evidenced today in the

Orthodox world, especially in Russia, is something for which the Living Lord must be profoundly thanked. The Catholics, under the eminent leadership of that remarkable man, John Paul II, are manifesting an immense vitality all over the world. But materially, politically, and morally, the Protestants of America command absolutely unprecedented resources, and spiritually they are in a state of creative ferment. In one brief sentence Billy Graham expressed this in his message on the occasion of the groundbreaking ceremony for this Center on September 28, 1977, when he said: "We have greater opportunities, greater challenges, greater needs than at any time in history."

What together, not separately but together, and in sincere cooperation with other Christians, the Protestants of America can do today for the promotion of the highest interests of man and the spirit, in the media, in the schools and universities, in the churches themselves, in the seminaries, in individual personal character, in popular literature, in the conduct of business, in the councils of the state, in international relations, and in the general quality of life of a whole epoch, is more, by far, than any other group of Christians can effect. And so the burden of their infinite accountability before God and history can only be carried at once with the deepest joy and the most authentic humility.

Protestantism emphasizes four fundamental truths: the supreme importance of the Bible, both Old and New Testaments, as the Word of God; Jesus Christ of

Nazareth as the Living Lord of lords and King of kings, with whom we must, and indeed we can, have a direct personal relationship; justification by faith and not by works, which is best expressed by Romans 4:5: "But to him that worketh not, but believeth on him that justifieth the ungodly, his faith is counted for righteousness"; and individual, personal, responsible freedom as the very essence of the dignity of man.

The year 1983 will mark the 500th anniversary of the birth of Martin Luther. During these five centuries the four basic affirmations of the Reformation have permeated the entire Christian world. Who among the faithful in all branches of Christianity today is not reading the Bible, or is prevented or discouraged from reading it? Who does not live, in some sense, in the presence of Jesus, the Living Lord? Who, knowing his own inveterate rottenness, and knowing it invariably precisely when he is at his best, expects to be saved by his sanctity only or by the merits of his works? And who is not placing freedom of thought, conscience, choice, and belief at the heart of all clamor for human rights? The Reformation has made its point.

Who therefore can predict today what may not be celebrated precisely on the occasion of the 500th anniversary of the birth of Martin Luther three years from now, in terms of closer understanding, and therefore mutual appreciation and forgiveness, between Protestantism on the one hand and Catholicism and Orthodoxy on the other? "O the depth of the riches both of the

21

wisdom and knowledge of God! how unsearchable are his judgments, and his ways past finding out! For who hath known the mind of the Lord, or who hath been his counselor?'' (Romans 11:33-34).

For the Protestants, therefore, to be able to fulfill their appointed destiny, now that their four distinctive emphases are universally accepted and absorbed, it would seem three requirements are necessary: greater unity among themselves (some of them are hardly on speaking terms with others); greater understanding and mutual toleration between the Evangelicals among them (although all Christians, by definition, are evangelical) and the more established churches; and rediscovering and appropriating the infinite riches of the great tradition: Orthodox, Catholic, and Protestant. On the first two points, Billy Graham, with his spirit and his name, and the Center named after him here, may be called to play a leading role.

On the third point, when Catholics sing in their churches, ''A Mighty Fortress is our God,'' as lustily as it is sung by the lustiest Lutherans, you feel we are already in a new age. Consequently I ask: who could possibly be harmed or impoverished, from the point of view of knowing and loving and worshiping Jesus Christ, if he knew something authentic about St. Ignatius of Antioch, or St. John Chrysostom, or St. Basil the Great, or St. Ephrem, or St. Augustine, or St. Thomas Aquinas, or St. Teresa of Avila? I assure you these are among the greatest Christians of all time, and Protestants will not be polluted if they steep themselves in them.

And yet there are people who are offended by the mere mention of the word "Saint," especially when written with a capital "S"! Having regard to the infinitely serious issues at stake, I trust this particular human offense will be transcended.

There are also some who affect to think that nothing really worth knowing happened in the Christian world between Saint Paul and Billy Graham. I know Billy Graham is a landmark, but not a landmark to the extent that everything between him and Saint Paul has been a total blank. Jesus Christ, who is the light of the world, will not be revealed as such, and His wonderful light will not shine in the awful darkness of our world, until the American Evangelicals, on whom so much depends today, integrate into themselves, and get themselves integrated into, the unity and continuity of the cumulative Christian tradition. He has shone on many a soul and many a culture in the past, and not only on the Evangelicals of today.

What could not be achieved for the glory of God and the name of Jesus Christ, and indeed for peace and understanding among all men, if the principle of freedom, which is of course sacred and primordial, did not obliterate or unduly interfere with the principle of solidarity and cooperation and mutual trust and forbearance, which is also primordial, and if the dimension of history is confidently opened wide and the cumulative tradition understood and loved and claimed? For us men in this vale of tears there is more than just God and the Bible and you as an individual person at this very moment: there are also others, both in time and space; and it is communion with others across the ages that is more sorely needed today than even communion with others in our time.

2

THIS IS THE SPIRITUAL SIDE of the problem; there is also the intellectual side.

In the nature of the case evangelization is always the most important task to be undertaken by mortal man. For proud and rebellious and self-sufficient man—and pride and rebellion and self-sufficiency are the same thing—to be brought to his knees and to his tears before the actual majesty and grace and power of Jesus Christ is the greatest event that can happen to any man. Indeed just as every man is ordained to die, so every man is ordained to this event happening in his own life. And those who are engaged in mediating this event, the evangelists, are the supreme heralds of God.

But just as we are not alone with God and the Bible but also with others, so we are not only endowed with a soul and a will to be saved but also with a reason to be sharpened and satisfied. This reason wonders about everything, including God, and we are to seek and love and worship the Lord our God with all our strength and all our mind. And because we are with others we are arguing and reasoning with one another all the time. Indeed every sentence and every discourse is a product of reason. And so it is neither a shame nor a sin to discipline and cultivate our reason to the utmost; it is a necessity, it is a duty, it is an honor to do so.

Therefore, if evangelization is the most important task, the task that comes immediately after it—not in the tenth place, nor even the third place, but in the second place—is not politics, nor economics, nor the quest of comfort and security and ease, but to find out exactly what is happening to the mind and the spirit in the schools and universities. And once a Christian discovers that there is a total divorce between mind and spirit in the schools and universities, between the perfection of thought and the perfection of soul and character, between intellectual sophistication and the spiritual worth of the individual human person, between reason and faith, between the pride of knowledge and the contrition of heart consequent upon being a mere creature, and once he realizes that Jesus Christ will find Himself less at home on the campuses of the great universities, in Europe and America, than almost anywhere else, he will be profoundly disturbed, and he will inquire what can be done to recapture the great universities for Jesus Christ, the universities which would not have come into being in the first place without Him.

The Two Tasks

What can the poor church, even at its best, do, what can evangelization, even at its most inspired, do, what can the poor family, even at its purest and noblest, do, if the children spend between fifteen and twenty years of their life, and indeed the most formative period of their life, in school and college in an atmosphere of formal denial of any relevance of God and spirit and soul and faith to the formation of their mind? The enormity of what is happening is beyond words.

The church and the family, each already encumbered with its own strains and ordeals, are fighting a losing battle, so far as the bearing of the university upon the spiritual health and wholeness of youth is concerned. All the preaching in the world, and all the loving care of even the best parents between whom there are no problems whatever, will amount to little, if not to nothing, so long as what the children are exposed to day in and day out for fifteen to twenty years in the school and university virtually cancels out, morally and spiritually, what they hear and see and learn at home and in the church. Therefore the problem of the school and university is the most critical problem afflicting Western civilization. And here we meet laughing and relaxing and enjoying ourselves and celebrating as though nothing of this order of gravity were happening!

I assure you, so far as the university is concerned, I have no patience with piety alone—I want the most rigorous intellectual training, I want the perfection of the mind; equally, I have no patience with reason alone—I want the salvation of the soul, I want the fear of the Lord, I want at least neutrality with respect to the knowledge of Jesus Christ.

What I crave to see is an institution that will produce as many Nobel Prize winners as saints, an institution in which, while producing in every field the finest works of thought and learning in the world, Jesus Christ will at the same time find Himself perfectly at home in it—in every dormitory and lecture hall and library and laboratory. This is impossible today. Why it is impossible, is the most important question that can be asked.

The sciences are flourishing as never before, and may they keep on flourishing and exploding and discovering!

And lest I be misunderstood, let me state at once that I consider Freiburg, the Sorbonne, Harvard, Princeton, and Chicago among the greatest—and some of them the greatest—universities in the world, and, provided my children qualify, I would certainly send them to them. The diversity and quality of the intellectual fare available to the student in these universities is absolutely unprecedented in history. Western civilization can be proud of many things; of nothing it can be more proud than of its great universities.

But I am worried about the humanities—about philosophy, psychology, art, history, literature, sociology, the interpretation of man as to his nature and his destiny. It is in these realms that the spirit, the fundamental attitude, the whole outlook on life, even for the scientist himself, are formed and set. Nor am I unaware and unappreciative of the great advances achieved in the methods, techniques and tools of education, and in the remarkable enlargement of the scope of the curriculum. But in terms of content and substance, what is the dominant philosophy in the humanities today?

We find on the whole and for the most part: materialism and hedonism; naturalism and rationalism; relativism and Freudianism; a great deal of cynicism and nihilism; indifferentism and atheism; linguistic analysis and radical obfuscation; immanentism and the absence of any sense of mystery, any sense of wonder, any sense of tragedy; humanism and self-sufficiency; the worship of the future, not of something above and outside and judging past, present, and future; the relative decay of the classics; the uncritical worship of everything new and modern and different; a prevailing false conception of progress; an uncritical and almost childish optimism; an uncritical and morbid pessimism; the will to power and domination. All of which are essentially so many modes of self-worship. Any wonder there is so much disorder in the world?!

If what I say is true, then as Christians you should not be able to sleep not only tonight but for a whole week. But I know you are going to sleep very soundly tonight, probably because you do not believe me, probably because you do not care!

At the heart of all the problems facing Western civilization—the general nervousness and restlessness, the dearth of grace and beauty and quiet and peace of soul, the manifold blemishes and perversions of personal character; problems of the family and of social relations in general, problems of economics and politics, problems of the media, problems affecting the school itself and the church itself, problems in the international order—at the heart of the crisis in Western civilization lies the state of the mind and the spirit in the universities.

It is totally vain, it is indeed childish, to tackle these problems as though all were well, in morals and in the fundamental orientation of the will and mind, in the great halls of learning. Where do the leaders in these realms come from? They all come from universities. What they are fed, intellectually, morally, spiritually, personally, in the fifteen or twenty years they spend in the school and university, is the decisive question. It is there that the foundations of character and mind and outlook and conviction and attitude and spirit are laid, and, to paraphrase a Biblical saying, if the wrong foundations are laid, or if the right foundations are vitiated or undermined, "what can the righteous do?" (Psalm 11:3).

Of course at this point the charge of self-righteousness will be leveled. But the question is so momentous that it must be vigorously raised even at the risk of this charge and of a dozen other charges and misunderstandings.

If there are three billion dollars to be thrown away—and, if not every day or every week, at least every month three billion dollars are being thrown away—let them go to founding and supporting some kind of institute whose sole aim is to find out the truth of what is happening in the humanities in the great universities of Europe and America.

The finest minds must be enlisted—philosophers, scientists, poets, theologians, preachers, Cardinals, Bishops, university presidents, presidents of republics, presidents of corporations—twenty at most and only five to begin with. They may include two or three non-Christians, but all the rest must be dedicated Christians. Their mandate is twofold: to produce by the end of this decade the most objective, exhaustive, and thorough study of what is really happening in the great universities of Europe and America in the field of the humanities, and to suggest practical ways and means for permeating that field with the right spirit, the right attitude, in a word, with right reason.

This is a Christian undertaking. Secularist-rationalist-humanist experimentation with liberal education is going on all the time, and only last year a great university put forward its own project. Christ being the light of the world, His light must be brought to bear on the problem of the formation of the mind. The investigation will have to be accomplished with the utmost discretion and humility, and it can only be carried out by men of prayer and faith. Once the light of Christ is shed on this study, incalculable will be the light the study itself will shed on all problems facing the Western world.

The thing is not mechanical nor is it a question of reforming the university; the university only reflects the mind of contemporary culture; we are dealing here with a thoroughgoing critique, from the point of view of Jesus Christ, of Western civilization as to its highest contemporary values. This is what lends this task its grandeur and its supreme responsibility.

I regret this is all abstract thinking, and nothing is more hateful to me than this kind of thinking. But I wanted only to pose the problem. Believe me, my friends, the mind today is in profound trouble, perhaps more so than ever before. How to order the mind on sound Christian principles at the very heart of where it is formed and informed, namely, in the universities, is one of the two greatest themes that can be considered. While we are living ''between the times,'' I mean, between the First and the Second Coming of Jesus Christ, and while human society continues to be under the sway of terrible sin and corruption, this theme must engage us with the utmost urgency.

The problem is not only to win souls but to save minds. If you win the whole world and lose the mind of the world, you will soon discover you have not won the world. Indeed it may turn out that you have actually lost the world.

In order to create and excel intellectually, must you sacrifice or neglect Jesus? In order to give all your life to Jesus, must you sacrifice or neglect learning and research? Is your self-giving to scholarship and learning essentially incompatible with your self-giving to Jesus Christ? These are the ultimate questions, and I beg you to beware of thinking that they admit of glib answers. I warn you: the right answers could be most disturbing.

Could the Billy Graham Center at Wheaton College sponsor this task? It remains to be seen whether it could. But if Christians do not care for the intellectual health of their own children and for the fate of their own civilization, a health and a fate so inextricably bound up with the state of the mind and spirit in the universities, who is going to care? The task is gigantic, and for it to be accomplished as I believe Christ Himself would want it to be accomplished, people must be set on fire for it. It is not enough to be set on fire for evangelization alone.

This is a solemn occasion. I must be frank with you: the greatest danger besetting American Evangelical Christianity is the danger of anti-intellectualism. The mind as to its greatest and deepest reaches is not cared for enough. This cannot take place apart from profound immersion for a period of years in the history of thought and the spirit. People are in a hurry to get out of the university and start earning money or serving the church or preaching the Gospel. They have no idea of the infinite value of spending years of leisure in conversing with the greatest minds and souls of the past, and thereby ripening and sharpening and enlarging their powers of thinking. The result is that the arena of creative thinking is abdicated and vacated to the enemy. Who among the Evangelicals can stand up to the great secular or naturalistic or atheistic scholars on their own terms of scholarship and research? Who among the Evangelical scholars is quoted as a normative source by the greatest secular authorities on history or philosophy or psychology or sociology or politics? Does your mode of thinking have the slightest chance of becoming the dominant mode of thinking in the great universities of Europe and America which stamp your entire civilization with their own spirit and ideas?

It will take a different spirit altogether to overcome this great danger of anti-intellectualism. As an example only, I say this different spirit, so far as the domain of philosophy alone is concerned, which is the most important domain so far as thought and intellect are concerned, must see the tremendous value of spending a whole year doing nothing except poring intensely over the *Republic* or the *Sophist* of Plato, or two years over the *Metaphysics* or the *Ethics* of Aristotle, or three years over the *City of God* of Augustine. Even if you start now on a crash program in this and other domains, it will be a century at least before you catch up with the Harvards and Tübingens and the Sorbonnes, and think of where these universities will be then! For the sake of greater effectiveness in witnessing to Jesus Christ Himself, as well as for their own sakes, the Evangelicals cannot afford to keep on living on the periphery of responsible intellectual existence.

In the short time allotted to me I am only here to intimate and point out: I am not to expound. But the real meat and marrow come only in the expounding.

Responsible Christians face two tasks—that of saving the soul and that of saving the mind. I am using soul and mind here without definition, but I can define them in precise, philosophical-theological terms. The mind is desperately disordered today. I am pleading that a tiny fraction of Christian care be extended to the mind too. If it is the will of the Holy Ghost that we attend to the soul, certainly it is not His will that we neglect the mind. No civilization can endure with its mind being as confused and disordered as ours is today. All our ills stem proximately from the false philosophies that have been let loose in the world and that are now being taught in the universities, and ultimately of course, as President Armerding observes in his book *Leadership* in another context, from the devil, whether or not the human agents knew it. Save the university and you save Western civilization and therewith the world.

What could be more wonderful than for a Center named after the greatest Evangelist of our age to aim at achieving, under God and according to God's own pace, the twofold miracle of evangelizing the great universities and intellectualizing the great Evangelical movement? These two things are absolutely impossible, and because they are at the same time absolutely needed, God can make them absolutely possible.

Every self-defeating attitude stems originally from the devil, because he is the adversary, the arch-nihilist *par excellence*. It cannot be willed by the Holy Ghost. Anti-intellectualism is an absolutely self-defeating attitude. Wake up, my friends, wake up: the great universities control the mind of the world. Therefore how can evangelism consider its task accomplished if it leaves the university unevangelized? And how can evangelism evangelize the university if it cannot speak to the university? And how can it speak to the university if it is not itself already intellectualized? Therefore evangelism must first intellectualize itself to be able to speak to the university and therefore to be able to evangelize the university and therefore to save the world. This is the great task, the historic task, the most needed task, the task required loud and clear by the Holy Ghost Himself, to which the Billy Graham Center must humbly address itself.

And if this should happen, then think of the infinite joy that would overflow our hearts. Future generations will bless your name and sing your praises for centuries to come. Who, then, would not join with David in singing: "Bless the Lord, O my soul: and all that is within me, bless his holy name. Bless the Lord, O my soul, and forget not all his benefits: . . . I will sing unto the Lord as long as I live: I will sing praise to my God while I have my being." (Psalm 103:1 & 2; and 104:33).

The Billy Graham Center, a division of Wheaton College, combines research and study in evangelism and world mission with scholarly excellence for service to the church and society. Its resources and programs bring the needs of the world to the scholars, and facilitate application of their knowledge to the issues of our day.

The emphasis of the Center is world evangelization. Beyond the primary task of proclaiming the good news of redemption, it focuses informed Christian concern and biblical principles on the crises of our age, especially those that affect the vitality of the church and the promotion of a society consistent with scriptural admonitions.

The special resources of the Center include extensive holdings in its archives, library, and museum. Evangelicals have been so busy "doing" that they have not taken the proper time to collect and analyze the records of their activity for application to contemporary situations. Each department of the Center, therefore, is designed to assist in this scholarship and to communicate the evangelical heritage in missions and evangelism. In addition, Center-sponsored programs and projects utilize the human and spiritual resources which include not only the Christian faculty of Wheaton College, but also visiting scholars, researchers, and experienced practitioners from around the world.

By fostering a better understanding of the past, the Center is dedicated to stimulating a vision of what God can do in the future through dedicated servants of Jesus Christ.

37